## Hello, Family Members,

Learning to read is one of the most important accomplishments of early childhood. **Hello Reader!** books are designed to help children become skilled readers who like to read. Beginning readers learn to read by remembering frequently used words like "the," "is," and "and"; by using phonics skills to decode new words; and by interpreting picture and text clues. These books provide both the stories children enjoy and the structure they need to read fluently and independently. Here are suggestions for helping your child *before*, *during*, and *after* reading:

### Before
- Look at the cover and pictures and have your child predict what the story is about.
- Read the story to your child.
- Encourage your child to chime in with familiar words and phrases.
- Echo read with your child by reading a line first and having your child read it after you do.

### During
- Have your child think about a word he or she does not recognize right away. Provide hints such as "Let's see if we know the sounds" and "Have we read other words like this one?"
- Encourage your child to use phonics skills to sound out new words.
- Provide the word for your child when more assistance is needed so that he or she does not struggle and the experience of reading with you is a positive one.
- Encourage your child to have fun by reading with a lot of expression . . . like an actor!

### After
- Have your child keep lists of interesting and favorite words.
- Encourage your child to read the books over and over again. Have him or her read to brothers, sisters, grandparents, and even teddy bears. Repeated readings develop confidence in young readers.
- Talk about the stories. Ask and answer questions. Share ideas about the funniest and most interesting characters and events in the stories.

I do hope that you and your child enjoy this book.

—Francie Alexander
Reading Specialist,
Scholastic's Learning Ventures

*For two dentists who make me smile,*
*Michael Axelrod and Joel Fischer*
*— B.K.*

*To Dr. Vogel and his wonderful staff*
*— S.B.*

The editors would like to thank Dr. Lawrence Golub for his expertise.

Library of Congress Cataloging-in-Publication Data

Katz, Bobbi.
  Make way for tooth decay / by Bobbi Katz; illustrated by Steve Björkman.
    p. cm. — (Hello reader! Science. Level 3)
  Summary: In rhyming verse, bacteria describe how they live in the mouth and cause plaque, cavities, and other problems.
  ISBN 0-590-52290-6
  1. Dental caries — Juvenile literature  2. Bacteria — Juvenile literature.  3. Teeth — Care and hygiene — Juvenile literature  4. Mouth — Care and hygiene — Juvenile literature.  [1. Teeth — Care and hygiene.]    I. Björkman, Steve, ill.
II. Title.  III. Series.
RK63.K38  1999
617.6'7 — dc21                                                    98-22397
                                                                       CIP
                                                                        AC
12  11  10  9  8  7  6  5  4  3              9/9  0/0  01  02  03  04

# MAKE WAY FOR TOOTH DECAY

by Bobbi Katz

Illustrated by Steve Björkman

Hello Reader! Science — Level 3

SCHOLASTIC INC.

New York  Toronto  London  Auckland  Sydney

What's in your mouth?
Are you sure you know?
Or maybe you don't care.

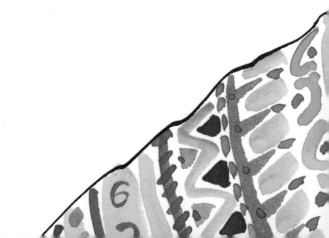

Well, there's more than teeth
and a long, pink tongue.
You have company in there.

Meet your guests.
We're called bacteria.
Your mouth is our cafeteria.

Teeny, tiny, out of sight,
we do our best to be polite.
"Pardon us!" is what we say.
"Please,
make way for tooth decay!"

We're bacteria.
We stay on track.
We work hard to build up plaque.

What is plaque?
A living glue made up of us
and food you chew.
Saliva's in the mixture, too.

What's saliva?
A big word for spit.
Your tongue would be dry
if you didn't have it.

But let's get back
to lovely plaque,
which sticks right
to your teeth.
It forms a shield
so cavities
can dig holes
underneath.

Water won't wash plaque away.
Hip, hip, hooray for tooth decay!

Bacteria, as you can see,
always go for quality.

How can you help us build up plaque?
*Never* miss a chance to snack —
candy, soda, cookies, sweets.
We'll do wonders with those treats.

When kids like you cooperate,
bacteria can celebrate.

As we bacteria multiply,
plaque thickens into goo.
*Never ever* brush your teeth.
Protect your plaque. Won't you?

Dentists claim they have the truth.
They've made a study of every tooth.
What's their motto?
  "Stop that plaque!
Mouthwash!
  Toothbrush!
   Let's attack."

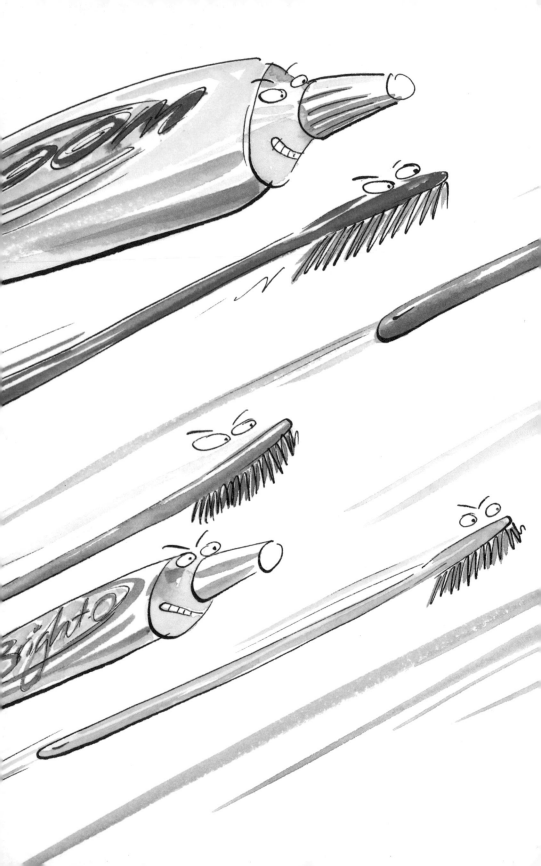

Mouthwash tastes yucky.
That's what we think.
Swish and spit!
We're down the sink.

Chocolate milk
has a yummy taste.
But mouthwash?
What an awful waste.

Toot! Toot! Toothbrush!
Stay away!
Please,
make way for tooth decay.

Dentists, we are at a loss.
You tell people floss, floss, floss!
That's not a friendly thing to do!

Someday, someone might floss you.

Your chairs provide a comfy ride.
Then what do you say?
**"Open wide!"**
Six-month checkups?
　X rays?
　　PLEASE!
You pick.
　You poke
　　and then…
charge fees.

We're so small.
We're so polite.
Kids, don't join
the dentists' fight.
Don't become our enemies!
We know you hear us.
**Listen, please!**

Depend on *us* to tell the truth:
Spare the care and rot the tooth!

Bacteria will *always* say,
"Please,
make way for tooth decay!"